Walks around Rosedale Abbey

Covering 554 square miles, the North York Moors National Park is one of England's finest landscapes. Heather moors, pastoral dales and a spectacular coastline give the area unique qualities that the Park Authority strives to protect and conserve.

Historical photographs from the Hayes Collection at the Ryedale Folk Museum.

Published by North York Moors National Park
© North York Moors National Park, 1998
ISBN 0 907480 70 5

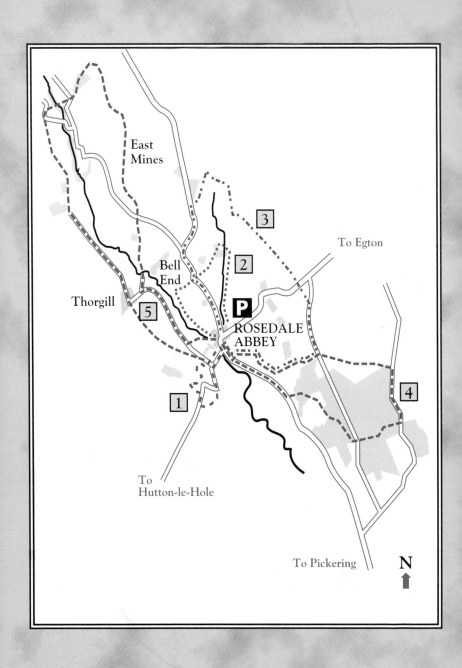

East
Mines

To Egton

Bell
End

Thorgill

ROSEDALE
ABBEY

To
Hutton-le-Hole

To Pickering

N

About this guide

Welcome to Rosedale, deep in the North York Moors National Park. This secluded valley boasts some of the finest walking country in the area. From high moorland views to shady forested paths, riverside ambles to picturesque farmsteads, there is much to explore and enjoy.

The five walks in this guide help you discover the stories behind this beautiful landscape. Take a stroll to the industrial remains of the 19th century or go in search of a long lost priory. Look for wildlife or discover how the landscape is cared for today. Whichever route you follow, Rosedale's story is compelling, sometimes destructive but always interesting.

The walks are all circular and vary from 2 to 7½ miles. The times suggested are generous - for people who prefer to amble rather than march. Some routes can be combined to make a longer walk. Each walk starts from the car park on the Egton Road behind the Milburn Arms. Please take care when walking on roads.

IMPORTANT - Make sure you take a waterproof and wear stout shoes whenever you walk in the countryside, as paths can be muddy and the weather can change rapidly. You should avoid walking on the moorland in bad weather, especially when misty.

Walk 1 MINES AND KILNS

For seventy years, the quiet rural bliss of Rosedale was destroyed by a thriving ironstone industry. Follow this walk and you can see some reminders of this era and the changes it brought to the landscape.

TRACES OF AN INDUSTRIAL PAST

Many of the rocks in the dale sides around you contain iron ore. Since Roman times people have dug for the ironstone but mining on a large scale began in 1856.

As you walk, look for traces of the old industry. The most impressive relics are the roasting kilns which you can see from the footpath near the top of Bank Top. Here the miners roasted the iron ore to remove impurities such as water and carbonic acid.

Vast quantities of ore were tipped into the kilns from the railway line above them. The ore was mixed with coal and the whole mixture was set alight. The process was called calcination and its purpose was to purify the iron and reduce its weight before it was carried by railway over the moors, initially to County Durham and later to Middlesbrough.

The iron industry brought many changes to the landscape.

Rosedale chimney:
the engine-house chimney of the West Mines was a landmark for miles around until it was demolished in 1972.

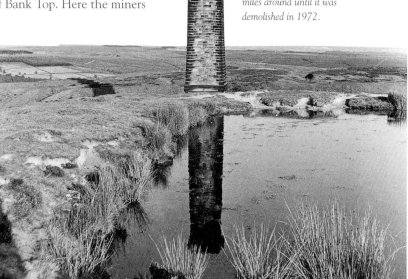

4

THE FIRST MINE

As you descend on the return journey of the walk you will have some excellent views over the site of the ironstone mine. The area above Hollins Farm was the first site to be mined on a large scale. To your right you can see the line of an old tramway. A steam engine at the top of the bank hauled wagons laden with ore up this tramway to the railway.

At its peak of production, the Hollins Farm mine yielded over 300,000 tonnes of ore a year. In 1874 it was abandoned, its reserves of iron having been exhausted in just 18 years.

Throughout this walk you can see rounded mounds on the hillside. These are spoil heaps left over from the mining operations. You will also pass a line of terraced houses which was built to provide homes for the railway workers.

SPOIL HEAPS

Take a look at the spoil heaps at the top of Bank Top. Much of it is loose and crumbly, with a red tinge to it. This is a clue that the spoil contains traces of iron. The changes brought by the iron industry provided new opportunities for wildlife. The loose nature of the spoil heaps makes them ideal places for rabbits to burrow and the area is now riddled with rabbit holes.

Walk 1

Bank Top

This walk follows footpaths up the side of the dale to Bank Top. The views are superb and you can see some of the remains of the old ironstone industry.

Time   1½ hours

Length   2 miles

Terrain A short walk with some steep slopes

1. Turn right out of the car park, then left on the road towards Pickering.

2. Turn right on to the Chimney Bank road.

3. After the bridge, take the footpath on the right alongside the house and follow the field edge up the hill.

4. Cross the road, go over the stile and follow the waymarked path through the golf course.

5. After climbing the ladder stile over the wall, turn left uphill. After the next wall and ladder stile, turn left alongside the wall.

6. Cross the stile and bear round to the right up the hill. Continue until you reach the track.

7. Turn left and follow the track behind the houses. After the last house cut down to the left, diagonally to the road.

8. Turn right along the road, then, at the footpath sign, turn left down the hillside to the fence then left along the fence.

9. At the track, turn left.

10. Continue along the road downhill and return to Rosedale.

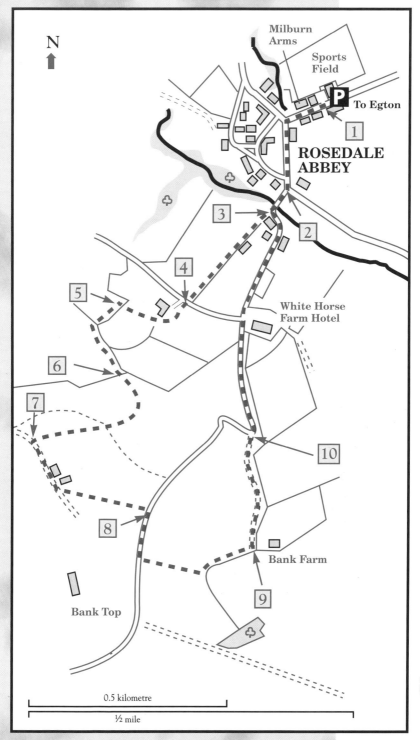

N

Milburn
Arms

Sports
Field

P

To Egton

1

ROSEDALE
ABBEY

3

2

4

5

6

7

White Horse
Farm Hotel

10

8

9

Bank Farm

Bank Top

0.5 kilometre

½ mile

Walk 2 ROSEDALE ABBEY

The origins of Rosedale Abbey lie in mediaeval times but in the Victorian era the village was transformed beyond recognition. This walk takes you through Rosedale Abbey, showing you how the village has changed over the years.

A VANISHED PRIORY

The name Rosedale Abbey suggests it was once the site of a mediaeval abbey. The "abbey" was actually a Cistercian priory, established in the 12th century to support a community of nine nuns and a prioress. The priory owned a lot of land in the area and managed large flocks of sheep. It was closed in 1535 following King Henry VIII's dissolution of the monasteries.

Today little remains of the priory. In the mid-19th century, it was pulled down to provide stone for new buildings in the village. The main remnant is a free-standing turret with a spiral staircase, which you can find in the grounds of the church. On a nearby hut is a weathered sundial which was taken from the priory.

Much of the stone from the priory was used to build the present church and if you look carefully you can find traces of the old convent. Look for the lintel above the north door which is made in the red stone of the priory and bears the words "Omnia Vanitas" (all is vanity). At the west end of the church are two trefoil heads which may be from the cloisters of the priory.

THE VICTORIAN REVOLUTION

Until the 18th century Rosedale Abbey was little more than a cluster of farms. Then the ironstone industry arrived and large numbers of people flooded to the area to work in the mines. New houses and shops were built to provide for this new community.

Look around the village today and it is easy to see that much of the village dates from the 19th century. Many of the buildings are in the typical Victorian style, with steeply angled roofs and large windows.

LIFE IN THE FAST STREAM

Much of this walk passes alongside fast flowing rivers and streams. Notice that there are no plants growing on the bed of the streams. The rapidly moving water washes away any sediment in the stream, leaving conditions unsuitable for plants.

The animals living in the streams are well suited to the fast flowing conditions. Insect larvae such as the nymphs of stoneflies and mayflies shelter in the gaps between the stones. If you are lucky you may see a dipper bobbing about in the water in search of insect prey.

Many of the trees growing by the water have round leaves and small green fruit. The trees are alder, a species which is specially adapted to live in wet conditions.

Walk 2

Bell End

A leisurely stroll, this route follows the River Seven before cutting across to Northdale and following the stream back to Rosedale Abbey.

Time	1½ hours
Length	2½ miles
Terrain	A gentle walk on footpaths through fields

1. Turn right out of the car park.

2. Go straight over at the crossroads and take the footpath, on the right, through the school playground past the remains of the Priory.

3. Turn right and take the second footpath on the left over the stone step stile behind the Old Police House. Turn right along the camp site road.

4. Go through the metal kissing gate and continue along the path through the fields.

5. After entering the small patch of trees, bear right uphill and follow the path to the road.

6. Turn left, then right past Bell End Farm.

7. Turn right along the footpath down into the valley.

8. Cross the bridge, then bear diagonally to the right up the hill.

9. Go through the gate and follow the waymarked path through the fields back to Rosedale Abbey.

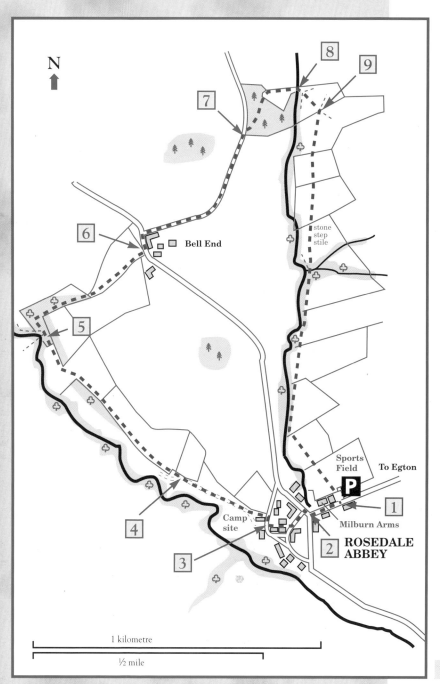

N

7

8

9

6   □ **Bell End**

stone
step
stile

5

4

**Sports
Field**

To Egton

P

1

**Camp
site**

Milburn Arms

2   **ROSEDALE
ABBEY**

3

1 kilometre

½ mile

Walk 3 WORKING THE LAND

With scattered farmsteads and a patchwork of fields, Rosedale owes much of its beauty to farming. This walk explores the farming landscape of Northdale and shows you how the area is cared for today.

CARING FOR THE COUNTRYSIDE

The economics and methods of modern farming threaten much that is special about this area. Yet Rosedale lies in the heart of the North York Moors National Park, a landscape that is specially conserved for the future. Today, the National Park Authority works with local farmers to manage the land and care for this superb countryside.

The North York Moors Farm Scheme was launched in 1990. It rewards farmers for the landscape and wildlife value of their land. In Northdale you can see some of the work carried out by farmers through

A CHANGING LANDSCAPE

Glance at the countryside around you and it is easy to see how traditional farming has shaped the area. Yet in recent decades farming has become a modern, high-tech industry, bringing many changes to the landscape.

One hundred years ago there were nine farms in Northdale. Today you will find just two working farmsteads. Developments in agriculture mean fewer people are needed to work the land and farming supports smaller communities. Disused buildings and crumbling ruins are the only reminders of the large rural populations of the past.

the Farm Scheme. The Scheme provides grants to help farmers repair drystone walls and maintain hedges, footpaths and traditional buildings. New woodlands have also been planted and existing native woods have been fenced off from livestock. This work will improve the landscape for many years to come.

If you look to the north, to Northdale Head, you can make out the remains of old fields high on the hillside. These fields are no longer profitable as pastures so they have been allowed to be reclaimed by the moorland.

ROUNDED HILLS

As you follow this walk, take a look at the rounded hill of Abbey Hill to the north of Rosedale Abbey. How was this land shape created?

Wind, rain and ice crafted the landscape. The top of Abbey Hill is a hard cap of ironstone or gritstone which is tough and resists erosion. Over thousands of years the softer rocks around it have weathered away, leaving an isolated, rounded hill.

Imagine what will happen to Bell Top in many years' time. At present it is joined to the rest of the moorland by a ridge of hard rock. But the ridge is narrower than the hilltop and it will erode faster than the rest of Bell Top. Eventually the ridge will be completely weathered away, leaving another isolated hill like Abbey Hill.

Walk 3

Northdale

This medium length walk takes you to the delightful dale of Northdale before climbing back over moorland. There are excellent views of lower Rosedale.

Time	3 hours
Length	5½ miles
Terrain	On roads and paths with a gradual climb up Northdale Rigg

1. From the car park, turn right into the village, then right again along the road towards Castleton.

2. Continue straight on, ignoring the road branching off to the right.

3. Bear right, signposted Castleton 10.

4. Turn right through the gate and follow the bridleway down to the left.

5. Go through the gate and continue down the track to the farm.

6. Go into the farmyard, then bear right between the barns.

7. Go down the field to cross the stream. Continue on up the side of the hill.

8. Turn right along the track, past Northdale Farm.

9. Turn left on the bridleway and follow it up the hill.

10. Go through the gate taking the right hand path across the moor. Turn right and follow the grassy track to the road.

11. Cross the road and follow the bridleway through the heather.

12. Turn right along the road.

13. Turn right and follow the footpath heading down across the moor.

14. Turn left through the gate. Continue down through the bracken and over the stile.

15. At the three-way signpost turn right and walk with the wall on your right. Cross the wall by the ladder stile and continue with the wall on your left.

16. Turn left through the farm and along the lane.

17. At the corner of the lane, follow the path through the kissing gate. Walk with the wall on your left, go through another gate, then bear diagonally across the field to the farm.

18. Go through the gate to the right of the barn and follow the track to the road. Turn right along the road to Rosedale Abbey.

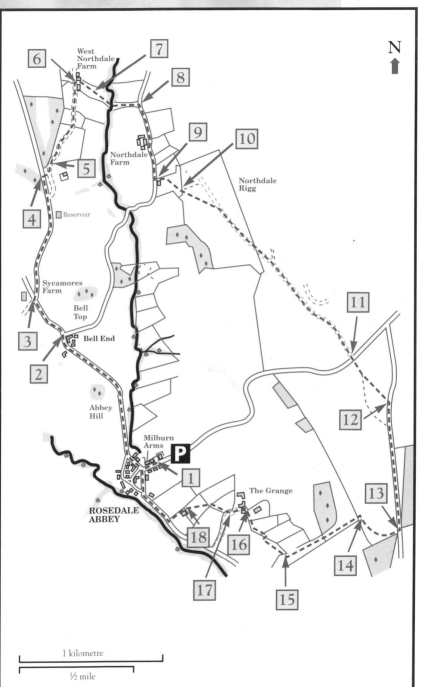

N

West
Northdale
Farm

6

7

8

Northdale
Farm

9

10

Northdale
Rigg

5

4

Reservoir

Sycamores
Farm

Bell
Top

3

Bell End

2

11

Abbey
Hill

12

Milburn
Arms

P

1

The Grange

13

ROSEDALE
ABBEY

18

16

14

17

15

1 kilometre

½ mile

Everywhere you look in Rosedale you see a landscape shaped by people. Nowhere is this more apparent than in the conifer plantations on the east of the dale. Follow this walk and you can discover how modern forestry has changed the countryside and how the wildlife has responded to this challenge.

A MAN-MADE FOREST

Almost a fifth of the North York Moors National Park is covered with conifer forests, mainly planted in the 1940s and 1950s on moorland areas. In the plantation on Hartoft Rigg you will see several types of tree. The only conifer trees which are native to Britain (although not Yorkshire!) are Scots pine, which are easy to recognise by their reddish bark. Many foreign tree species have also been planted, including larch, Norway spruce and Sitka spruce. They have all been chosen because they grow rapidly and produce good quality timber.

The conifer plantation is a working woodland, managed for a variety of purposes. As well as yielding a crop of timber, the Forestry Commission's conifer forests are important homes for wildlife and beautiful areas for people to explore and enjoy.

NEW OPPORTUNITIES

Notice that the trees vary in age throughout the forest, from fully grown to recently planted. There are also areas where the trees have been felled. This mosaic of age structure provides a whole range of opportunities for wild animals and plants.

Some of the richest habitats in the forest are the open strips of land beside roads, bridleways and forest tracks. Wildflowers such as harebells live in the drier areas,

S

MOORLAND

Later in this walk you will pass through heather moorland, another landscape created by people. Heather has grown on the moors since bronze age times. Today, the moors are used for sheep farming and to support populations of red grouse for shooting.

Look for patches where the heather has been burned. This shows how the moorland is managed. Burning kills grasses and other plants, but the heather quickly grows from underground shoots. This management produces a patchwork of tall heather where grouse nest and younger shoots for the grouse to feed on.

whilst you can find all sorts of ferns in darker and damper conditions.

In areas where the trees have been felled you can see heather, bilberry and grasses. These moorland plants are a reminder that the forests were originally planted on moorland. The plants survived as seeds in the ground when the area was covered by trees. Now they are springing to life in the lighter conditions.

The nightjar is one bird to benefit from the extensive tracts of conifer plantations. These migratory birds often nest on the ground in recently felled patches of forest. The best time to see them is at dusk, when they glide through open areas searching for insect prey.

17

Walk 4

Hartoft Rigg

This walk helps you explore the depths of a conifer forest. Look out for woodland wildlife along the way.

Time	3 hours
Length	5½ miles
Terrain	On roads and forest paths with a steady climb around Hartoft Rigg

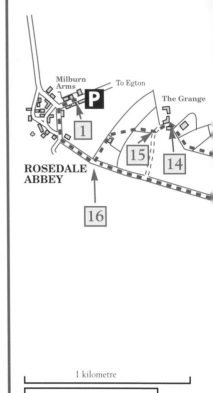

© Crown Copyright. NYMNP LA 08904L/98/03

1. Turn right out of the car park, then left along the main road out of the village. Continue for 1½ miles.

2. Turn left along the bridleway. Cross the field to the gate opposite.

3. Follow the path up through the forest. At the fork, bear right.

4. Go through the gate and cross the field, passing to the right of the farm house. Continue through two gates.

5. Turn left along the field edge to the track. Turn right along the track.

6. At the end of the drystone wall, follow the bridleway diagonally left ahead through the forest.

7. Turn left along the track, then right along the road. Turn left along the bridleway.

8. At the crossroads, follow the grassy bridleway ahead down the hill, walking to the right of the crumbling wall.

9. At the farm, turn left along the road.

10. Turn left along the bridleway. Go through the gate and walk straight ahead across the moor.

11. Go through the gate in the corner and cross the road. Follow the footpath heading down across the moor.

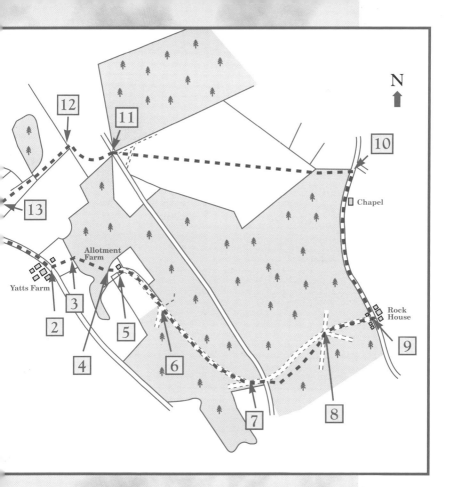

N

12
11
10
13
Chapel
Allotment
Farm
Yatts Farm
3
Rock
House
2
5
9
4
6
7
8

12. Turn left through the gate. Continue downhill through the bracken and over the stile.

13. At the three-way signpost turn right and walk with the wall on your right. Cross the wall by the ladder stile and continue with the wall on your left to the farm.

14. Turn left through the farm and along the lane.

15. At the corner of the lane, follow the path through the kissing gate. Walk with the wall on your left, go through another gate, then bear diagonally across the field to the farm.

16. Go through the gate to the right of the barn and follow the track to the road. Turn right along the road and return to Rosedale Abbey.

Walk 5 THE EAST MINES

Today Rosedale is a peaceful rural dale in the heart of the North York Moors National Park. In the 19th century it was part of industrial Yorkshire, with mines, kilns and a moorland railway. This route takes you deep into Rosedale where you can see reminders of the industrial age.

In 1860, people opened up mines on the eastern side of the dale to extract deposits of iron ore. The two sets of calcining kilns are easily visible where the miners roasted the ore to remove impurities.

A MOORLAND RAILWAY

Look for the line of the railway, which runs along the edge of the dale high on the valley sides. It was built to provide access to the mines, winding over the moors to Battersby Junction. This gave access

to County Durham and, later, to Middlesbrough. It is amazing to imagine the skill and efforts of the people who crafted this railway, over such wild and difficult terrain.

The railway served two purposes. It carried away the processed iron ore and brought coal from Durham to use in the kilns. The final stage of this walk takes you along part of the railway past the kilns. The railway branches into two levels. The upper line led to the mines above the kilns whilst the lower one served the kilns.

N.B. Please stay on the main lower railway. This is not a Public Right of Way but access is permitted as part of a Management Agreement between the landowner and the National Park Authority.

A DALE TRANSFORMED

From the railway you get superb views of Rosedale. During the mining period the population of the dale increased rapidly, from 558 to 2,839 in just 20 years. Look for terraces of houses in the dale. They were built in the latter days of the industry to provide homes for the miners. The railway men, however, were of a higher social class. They occupied homes built close to the mines and you can still see their ruined remains.

The eastern mines finally closed in 1926. Today the kilns are an impressive relic from this industrial era. The National Park Authority works with the landowner and English Heritage to conserve these valuable features for future generations to discover.

STONE TRODS

During this walk you will pass several stretches of path paved with stone slabs. Such stone trods are common throughout the North York Moors and they could be hundreds of years old.

The oldest trods date from mediaeval times, when monks travelled extensively through the area. Most of the paths are more recent, dating from the 18th and 19th centuries when all sorts of industries sprang up in the region.

It is easy to see how stone trods made an ideal surface for travelling. The single line of slabs was well suited for a farmer or monk to walk through the area. Trains of packhorses would also use them, by walking in single file.

Walk 5

Dale Head

Taking you right to the head of Rosedale, this route brings you back along the dismantled railway to the impressive ruins of the ironstone kilns.

Time	5 hours
Length	7½ miles
Terrain	A long gentle walk

1. Turn right out of the car park.

2. Go straight over at the crossroads and take the footpath, on the right, through the school playground past the remains of the Priory. Cross the road and take the path opposite, through the kissing gate. Cross straight over the camp site road and continue along the path.

3. Go over the footbridge and along the stone trod diagonally across the field.

4. Turn right at the road.

5. Turn left along the path across the fields.

6. Turn right, then left along the road through Thorgill.

7. Continue ahead.

8. Where the track descends to the right, carry straight on; diagonally up. Cross the stone step stile and continue to Moorlands Farm.

9. Go through the gate, turn right then left. Follow the track to Hollin Bush Farm.

10. At the farmyard take the footpath on the right, by crossing the stone step stile and cut diagonally across the field. Cross the footbridge and continue to the road.

11. Turn left along the road. Just before the farm take the bridleway on the right, go through the gate and up the hill alongside the stream.

12. Turn right along the dismantled railway. *Note: do not wander from the railway, as parts of this old industrial area are dangerous.*

13. Follow the path to the left of the buildings. Go through the gate and bear right down to the road.

14. Cross the road and follow the footpath opposite.

15. At the gate, bear right over the fields to the stream.

16. Cross the footbridge, go through the farmyard to the road. Turn left.

17. Turn left down the footpath and over the bridge. Turn right to return to Rosedale Abbey.

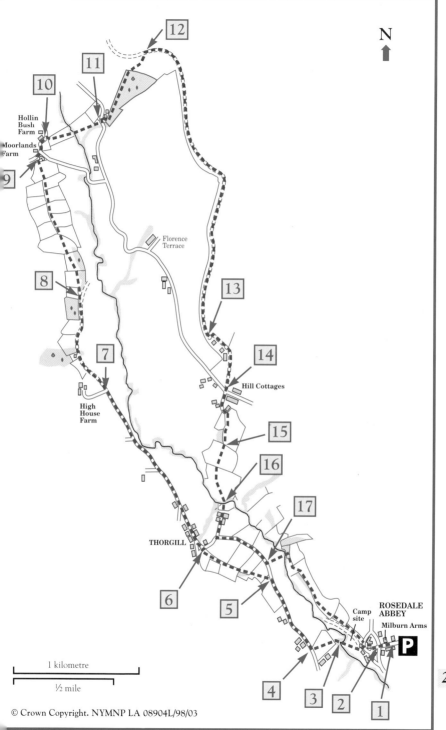

N

Hollin Bush Farm

Moorlands Farm

Florence Terrace

High House Farm

Hill Cottages

THORGILL

Camp site

ROSEDALE ABBEY

Milburn Arms

P

1 kilometre

½ mile

© Crown Copyright. NYMNP LA 08904L/98/03

MOORS MESSAGE

Tread Gently
- despite surviving all sorts of weather, the moors, their plants and animals are fragile and sensitive.

Fences & Walls
- keep some animals in and some out. Use stiles or gates (and shut them).

Fire
- uncontrolled fires can devastate vast areas of moorland which may never fully recover. Don't start campfires or drop cigarettes or matches.

Litter
- is dangerous as well as unsightly. Take it home.

Dogs
- keep dogs on leads at all times. A loose dog running over the moors can be catastrophic for sheep, ground nesting birds, and sometimes the dog itself.

Courtesy
- the North York Moors is a home and place of work for many people. Please respect their privacy.

Noise
- moorlands should be quiet places. Try to keep it that way.

Safety
- weather conditions can change quickly. Are you fully equipped?

Footpaths
- are for feet. Bicycles may be ridden on bridleways. Motorcycles and other traffic should stick to roads.

Leave the countryside
as you found it,
for others to enjoy.